MOVERS, SHAKERS, & HISTORY MAKERS

BOYAN SLAT
PIONEERING THE OCEAN CLEANUP

BY ISAAC KERRY

CAPSTONE PRESS
a capstone imprint

Capstone Captivate is published by Capstone Press, an imprint of Capstone.
1710 Roe Crest Drive
North Mankato, Minnesota 56003
www.capstonepub.com

Library of Congress Cataloging-in-Publication Data
Names: Kerry, Isaac, author.
Title: Boyan Slat : pioneering the ocean cleanup / by Isaac Kerry.
Description: North Mankato, Minnesota : Capstone Press, [2021] |
Series: Movers, shakers, and history makers | Includes bibliographical references and index. | Audience: Ages 8-11 | Audience: Grades 4-6 |
Summary: "Dutch student Boyan Slat always loved inventing. A visit to the oceans of Greece inspired his greatest invention ever. Why were there more plastic bags than fish? How could he save the sea? Learn more about Boyan's Great Pacific Garbage Patch project, The Ocean Cleanup; his plastic cleanup invention, System 001; and the challenges behind removing trash from our oceans and rivers"
Identifiers: LCCN 2020037999 (print) | LCCN 2020038000 (ebook) | ISBN 9781496695833 (hardcover) | ISBN 9781496697141 (paperback) | ISBN 9781977153906 (ebook pdf) |
Subjects: LCSH: Slat, Boyan—Juvenile literature. | Marine debris—Cleanup—North Pacific Ocean—Juvenile literature. | Marine pollution—Juvenile literature. | Plastic marine debris—Environmental aspects—Juvenile literature.
Classification: LCC TD427.M35 K47 2021 (print) | LCC TD427.M35 (ebook) |
DDC 628.1/68092—dc23
LC record available at https://lccn.loc.gov/2020037999
LC ebook record available at https://lccn.loc.gov/2020038000

Image Credits
Getty Images: East Bay Times/Digital First Media/Ray Chavez, cover (front); NOAA: 24; The Ocean Cleanup: 5, 22, 25, 27, 28, 30–31, 34, 35, 37, 40, 41, 42, Pierre Augier, 19, 33, Yuri van Greenen, 17; Shutterstock: Alba_alioth, 8, Andrei Dubadzel, cover (background), 1, Frank Cornelissen, 15, Frans Blok, 39, Imagine Earth Photography, 21, Peteri, 11, Roman Safonov, 7, setthayos sansuwansri, 12, Yevheniia Pavlovska, 13

Editorial Credits
Editor: Mari Bolte; Designer: Bobbie Nuytten; Media Researcher: Svetlana Zhurkin; Production Specialist: Katy LaVigne

All internet sites appearing in back matter were available and accurate when this book was sent to press.

TABLE OF CONTENTS

Words in **bold** are in the glossary.

CHAPTER ONE

ENDLESS INVENTIONS

Every generation has visionary leaders. These people help us see the world differently and push us to do more than we thought was possible. The 20th century had its share of visionaries, including Martin Luther King Jr., Albert Einstein, Helen Keller, and Steve Jobs. It's the 21st century, and new leaders are taking the stage. Many people think Boyan Slat is one of those leaders.

MORE PLASTIC THAN FISH

Boyan Slat was born in the city of Delft in the Netherlands on July 27, 1994. His mother was a consultant who helped people moving to the Netherlands. His father was an artist. They divorced when Boyan was a baby, and his father moved to his native Croatia.

Boyan on the floater of his first cleanup system in April 2018

Young Boyan loved inventing and making things like treehouses and ziplines with his friends. As he got older, he started working on harder projects like homemade rockets, and he began tinkering with computers.

In 2010, 16-year-old Boyan took a trip to Greece to go diving. What he saw there would change his life. He was hoping to swim with colorful fish and other beautiful sea creatures. Instead he found a sea filled with plastic. There were so many bags floating in the water one of his friends thought they were jellyfish. Surrounded by all this plastic, Boyan thought, "Why can't we clean this up?"

FACT

When Boyan was 14, he wanted to set a Guinness World Record. He launched 213 water rockets, the most ever set off at one time. "The experience taught me how to get people crazy enough to do things you want, and how to approach sponsors," he said later.

Boyan first discovered plastic pollution when diving in the Mediterranean Sea in Greece.

LEARNING MORE

Back at school, Boyan was assigned a research paper. He could choose any subject. Boyan decided to study plastic **pollution** in the ocean. Why was no one cleaning it up?

Boyan discovered that plastic pollution is a huge problem all over the world. Humans create more than 272 million metric tons of plastic each year. Half of this plastic is for single-use items, like water bottles and take-out containers.

One million plastic bottles are bought every minute around the world. That's about 17,000 per second.

HOW MUCH IS 8 MILLION TONS?

- 90 WASHINGTON MONUMENTS
- 300 STATUES OF LIBERTY
- 70,000 BLUE WHALES
- 1,000,000 TYRANNOSAURUS REXES
- 4,500,000 CARS
- 150,000,000 TOILETS
- 2,000,000,000 CATS

FACT

Every year, more than 8 million metric tons of plastic ends up in the ocean. Experts predict that there will be more plastic than fish in the ocean by 2050.

Tons of plastic pollution end up in the sea. Swirling ocean currents called **gyres** gather some of this trash into huge garbage patches. There are five major garbage patches in the world, but the largest is known as the Great Pacific Garbage Patch. It is more than twice the size of Texas and contains more than 1.8 trillion pieces of plastic. It has about 250 pieces of plastic for every person who is alive today.

Plastic can cause many problems for ocean creatures and humans. Some animals eat the plastic and can choke on it or get sick. Others, like dolphins and sea turtles, get tangled in it and die.

Plastic that stays in the ocean for longer periods of time can start to break down into **microplastics**. These tiny pieces of plastic are eaten by fish, that are eventually eaten by humans or large predators.

FACT

The Great Pacific Garbage Patch was discovered in 1997. **Oceanographer** Charles Moore found it while he was returning from a yacht race.

Some experts believe humans **ingest** 8.8 ounces (250 grams) of plastic every year without realizing it. That's enough to fill a dinner plate. Those tiny bits of plastic can leave harmful chemicals in our bodies or cause other problems with their presence.

TOP 10 SOURCES OF OCEAN'S PLASTIC WASTE

CHINA

EGYPT

BANGLADESH

VIETNAM

THAILAND

PHILIPPINES

NIGERIA

SRI LANKA

MALAYSIA

INDONESIA

Bundles of plastic bottles are prepared for recycling process.

Boyan learned that many scientists and **activists** were worried about plastic pollution. But they focused on stopping new plastic from coming into the ocean. Everyone thought that it would be too much work to clean up the plastic that was already there. Some estimates said it would take 79,000 years to remove.

The problem fascinated Boyan. He loved a challenge. Working on something everyone else thought couldn't be done made it even more exciting. He started brainstorming ideas of how to do the impossible.

HOW LONG DOES IT TAKE PLASTIC TO BREAK DOWN?

Plastic bag:
20 years

Plastic silverware:
100 years

Plastic straw:
200 years

Plastic cup:
400 years

Plastic bottle:
450 years

Plastic toothbrush:
500 years

CHAPTER TWO

GOING VIRAL

Boyan graduated from high school in 2012. He was headed to the Delft University of Technology as an aerospace engineering student. But first, he was invited to present his ideas about ocean cleanup at a TEDx conference.

TED TALKS

TED stands for Technology, Education, and Design. These conferences feature speakers who talk about big ideas and exciting new technologies. TEDx Talks give speakers the chance to present well-formed ideas in under 18 minutes. Sometimes they include tech demos, performances, or presentations of art. Some Talks are as short as 5 minutes. All past presentations can be found online—including Boyan's original talk.

Aerospace engineering building at Delft University of Technology in the Netherlands

The solution Boyan had dreamed up involved floating platforms that looked like huge spaceships. The device used the ocean's waves to move itself and gather up plastics. Everything on the platforms, including lights and electronics, was solar powered.

Boyan named his device the Ocean Cleanup **Array**. These arrays would be anchored to the ocean floor. As the ocean currents moved, the trash around the array would be captured by the platforms. After it was full of trash, a ship would come and bring the garbage to shore. The recycled ocean plastic would help pay for the array. "Working with nature instead of trying to fight it," he said later.

It was an interesting idea, but no one stepped forward to back the project. But Boyan couldn't stop thinking about it. After a few months of college, Boyan made the decision to drop out. He founded his own **nonprofit** organization and called it The Ocean Cleanup. His starting fund was just 300 euros of his own savings.

Boyan at his Ocean Cleanup office in 2016. Since he started his nonprofit in 2013, his staff has grown to more than 80 employees.

FACT

The euro is the currency of the European Union. In 2012, 300 euros would have been worth a little less than $400.

Boyan felt that no one else was trying to solve the problem—and that the problem got worse every year. He wanted to learn more. He spent his time interviewing researchers and other experts. He had a list of questions that would need to be answered to see if his idea would work.

In March 2013, things started to turn around for The Ocean Cleanup. Some news sites saw his TED talk. They shared it, and Boyan went viral. He was soon being called day and night for interviews by reporters all over the world. Boyan launched a **crowdfunding** campaign to get The Ocean Cleanup off the ground. He raised $90,000 and was able to hire a team of smart people to help make his dream a reality.

FACT

In 2014, Boyan was given the Champion of the Earth Award from the United Nations Environment Programme. He was the youngest person ever to receive it.

The video of Boyan's original TED talk has more than 3 million views on YouTube. He continued to talk about his cause at many press events.

CHAPTER THREE

STARTING THE CLEANUP

The first thing The Ocean Cleanup did was perform a feasibility study. This would see if the arrays could work. Almost 100 scientists and engineers volunteered to help read over Boyan's proposal. They wrote a huge 500-page report called "How the Oceans Can Clean Themselves."

The report found that Boyan's idea was possible: With enough arrays, almost half the Great Pacific Garbage Patch could be cleaned in only 10 years. The study also looked at possible negative environmental impacts of removing the trash. Even though the ocean would be a better place without the plastic, the cleanup had to be done carefully or sea life could be hurt.

Marine animals like humpback whales are hurt by ocean pollution. It's important that cleanup systems are safe for them.

Boyan in 2016 at an event showing an early version
of his system

Boyan estimated that each array would cost almost $5 million. To raise money, he started sending letters to companies. He described The Ocean Cleanup's vision. Then he asked for their help. No one wanted to contribute.

Boyan knew how important his work was. He refused to let a lack of funding stop him. He again turned to everyday people to help bring his vision to life. Now that he had a detailed study backing up his idea, he ran another crowdfunding campaign.

FACT

Boyan sent more than 300 emails looking for a sponsor. He only received one response—and it was to tell him why his plan was terrible.

The campaign was a huge success. More than 38,000 people gave $2 million toward the project. Additionally, several wealthy **philanthropists** stepped in. This let The Ocean Cleanup move on to the next step of their plan: creating the first real map of the Great Pacific Garbage Patch.

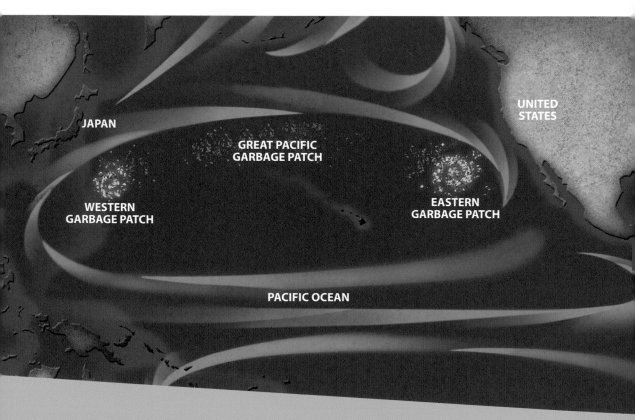

The Great Pacific Garbage Patch is also called the "Subtropical Convergence Zone." It is one of many garbage patches in our global ocean.

Boyan presenting the next phase of his project in May 2017

CHAPTER FOUR

STUDYING THE PROBLEM

Before they could start building anything, The Ocean Cleanup needed to learn more about the Great Pacific Garbage Patch. Everyone knew where it was, but no one had mapped it fully. Boyan also wanted to know exactly what kind of plastic made up the patch.

In August 2015, The Ocean Cleanup launched the Mega Expedition. Around 30 ships sailed to the patch. They took samples of the plastic they found there. This was the largest research expedition to take place on the open sea.

The Mega Expedition crew deploys a trawl to sample plastic pollutants.

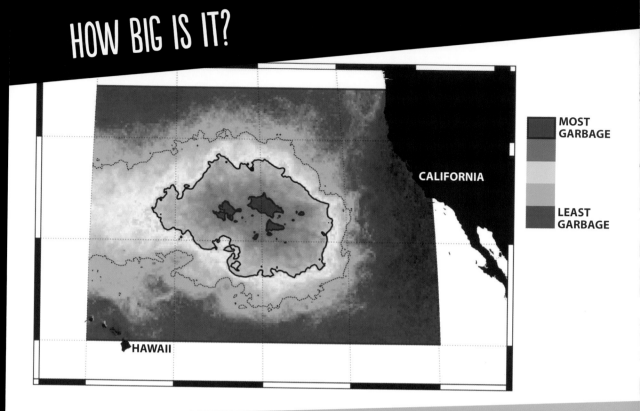

MOST
GARBAGE

CALIFORNIA

LEAST
GARBAGE

HAWAII

The Ocean Cleanup estimates the Great Pacific Garbage Patch is the size of 14,000 football fields.

The team found the patch was much bigger than anyone had thought. They also found that more than 90 percent of the plastic was still large enough to be easily removed. Amazingly, almost half of the trash they found was discarded fishing nets.

GHOST FISHING

Nets and other fishing supplies that get lost or abandoned at sea are known as ghost gear. These items make up almost 10 percent of all new plastic entering the ocean. They can last for up to 600 years before breaking down. They are especially dangerous to ocean life, which can get seriously hurt or die because of eating or getting caught in them.

STARTING THE TESTS

The information found by the Mega Expedition was just what Boyan and his engineers needed to get to work. They started developing **prototypes** of the systems they would use to clean up the trash.

The design of the cleanup system had now changed quite a bit from Boyan's original idea. A more flexible floating line, or "boom," had been added. It would be connected to netting that floated beneath the waves. The netting would be more durable than a large platform. It would also be able to avoid being damaged by the high waves of the Pacific Ocean.

The first prototype was launched in 2016. It was set in the dangerous waters of the North Sea, off the coast of the Netherlands. The waves and currents here were even stronger than in the Pacific.

After two months at sea, the test system started showing some damage. Boyan's team had to pull it back to shore.

The Ocean Cleanup team tests the system in the North Sea.

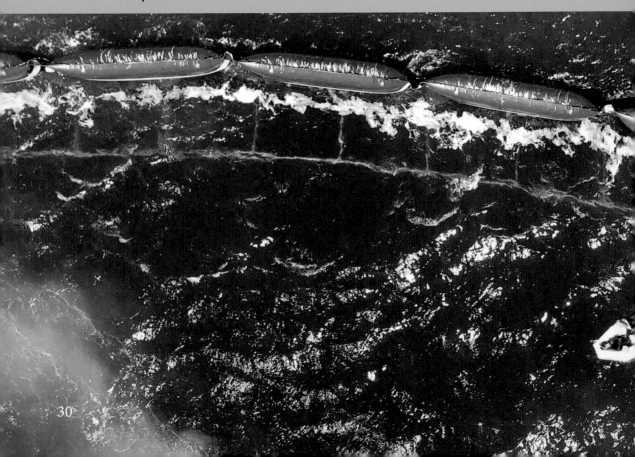

Instead of seeing the test as a setback, they treated it as a learning opportunity. Being able to look over the test system let them make an important discovery. They found that it would work better if it wasn't anchored to the ocean floor. Their updated design used giant underwater parachutes that slowed down the system. Hopefully, this would allow the system to capture plastic better and also not get damaged as easily.

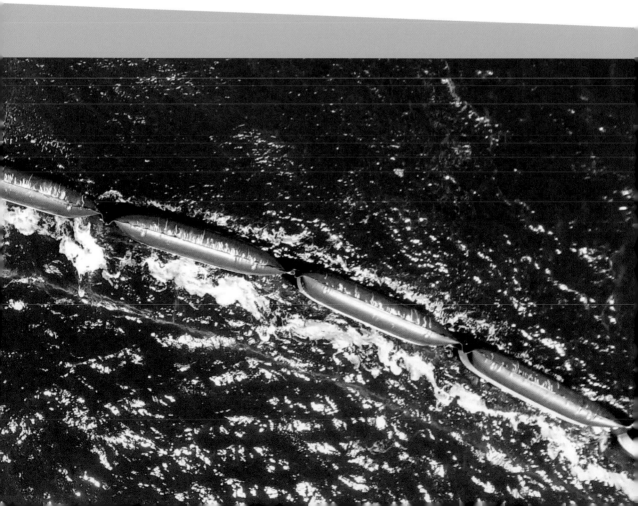

Boyan's team used the information from their prototypes and kept making improvements. Finally in 2018, Boyan was ready to show the world what The Ocean Cleanup had been working on. The new cleanup platform was named System 001. It launched from San Francisco and was towed to the Great Pacific Garbage Patch. Its mission was to prove to the world that The Ocean Cleanup's technology would work.

OVERCOMING SETBACKS

Soon after System 001 arrived at the garbage patch, it was clear something wasn't right. Plastic would be caught by the system, but the strong ocean waves would easily wash it away. While the team worked hard trying to fix this, a huge section of the boom broke off. After only four months at sea, the mission had to be canceled. The broken system was towed back to shore.

System 001 leaves San Francisco for the Great Pacific Garbage Patch in 2018.

Many people wondered if Boyan would ever succeed. They wrote about how he had made big promises but could not actually follow through. But Boyan believed in his project. He was determined to learn what he could and make the next versions of the system better.

The Ocean Cleanup crew inspects the plastics the system collected.

Boyan and his engineers spent the next five months working even harder to find out what went wrong. They created a new test platform named System 001/B. This latest system had several **modular** parts that could be switched out to test which part worked better. All these tests paid off. System 001/B successfully captured and held onto the plastic that floated into it. In December 2019, the first batch of plastic retrieved from the garbage patch was brought back to shore in Canada. The collected garbage filled 2,112 cubic-foot (60 cubic-meter) bags.

System 001/B undergoes a tow test in 2019.

CHAPTER FIVE

WHAT'S NEXT?

The team members at The Ocean Cleanup are moving into the next decade excited about what they are achieving. They are taking the lessons they have learned from all their tests and building a new and improved System 002. This will be the version of the cleanup platform they'll use on a large scale.

Plans for a dozen more Systems are standing by—once they secure the funding. Boyan hopes for a fleet of 60 of these platforms. They will work together to clean up the Great Pacific Garbage Patch. The plastic they bring to shore will be used to create products that will be sold to help pay for the cleanup. Boyan's goal is to use all the plastic they recover and not send any to a landfill.

Boyan in Vancouver, Canada, in 2019 explains how the collected plastic will be turned into products to sell to help fund future cleanups.

IT'S MADE OF WHAT?

Companies are already using recycled ocean plastics to create new things. Some items include:

- SUNGLASSES

- SHOES

- BAGS

- PACKAGING FOR BEAUTY SUPPLIES

- CLOTHING

- SKATEBOARDS

- TABLEWARE, SUCH AS PLATES, CUPS, AND VASES

While work was continuing on perfecting the ocean cleanup system, Boyan was thinking of the bigger picture. How could he solve the problem of new plastic coming into the sea? In 2017, The Ocean Cleanup started testing the Interceptor. This solar-powered platform floats on rivers and catches garbage before it can ever get to open water. These platforms can remove more than 50 metric tons of plastic every day.

The Interceptor docked in Rotterdam, the Netherlands, near the Maritime Museum

Boyan's goal is to place Interceptors in every highly polluting river in the world. This will let The Ocean Cleanup attack the plastic problem at both ends, by reducing new trash and removing trash that is already there. Boyan's goal for his organization is to remove 90 percent of all floating plastic in the ocean by 2040.

Boyan aboard the Interceptor on the Klang River in Malaysia

FACT

Eventually, all rivers lead to the ocean. Around 1,000 rivers in the world are responsible for 80 percent of new plastic that flows into the ocean.

The Ozama River in Santo Domingo, Dominican Republic, awaited its cleanup by the Interceptor in 2020.

The Ocean Cleanup team's goal is to clean up the 1,000 most polluting rivers all over the world within five years.

Boyan Slat broke a Guinness World Record at age 14. He founded his own company and gave a TED talk at 18. In 2017, he was chosen as Reader's Digest's European of the Year. In 2019, the European Commission appointed Boyan a board member of its ocean mission. He continues to be recognized for his knowledge and achievements.

But his journey started in a quite simple way: He found a problem and went searching for a solution. Like so many other visionaries, he didn't let popular opinion stop him from trying to do the impossible. Boyan doesn't know exactly what the future holds for him or what his next project will be. He does know that he wants to keep tackling big problems and help make the world a better, cleaner place.

TIMELINE

1994: Boyan Slat is born

2010: Boyan takes a diving trip to Greece where he sees more plastic than fish

2012: Boyan presents his TEDx Talk entitled "How the Oceans Can Clean Themselves"

2013: Boyan drops out of college and founds The Ocean Cleanup

Boyan's TED Talk goes viral and The Ocean Cleanup launches its first crowdfunding campaign

2014: "How the Oceans Can Clean Themselves" study is published

Boyan launches second crowdfunding campaign and raises more than $2 million

2015: The Ocean Cleanup launches the Mega Expedition to map the Great Pacific Garbage Patch

2016: Boyan and his engineers start testing prototypes of their cleanup systems

2017: The Ocean Cleanup starts testing its Interceptor river cleaning platform

2018: System 001 is launched in the Great Pacific Garbage Patch; it breaks apart and must be towed back to land

2019: The Ocean Cleanup launches the new and improved System 001/B, which successfully captures plastic and returns to shore

GLOSSARY

activist (AK-tuh-vihst)
a person who works for social or political change

array (uh-RAY)
a large group of items placed in a certain order

crowdfunding (KROWD-fuhn-ding)
a fundraising system in which many people each donate a small amount of money

gyre (GUY-uhr)
a system of circulating ocean currents

ingest (in-JEST)
to consume a substance by swallowing or absorbing it

microplastic (MY-kroh-plass-tik)
any type of plastic fragment less than 0.2 inch (5 millimeters) in length

modular (MAH-juh-luhr)
made up of several separate pieces or sections

nonprofit (nahn-PRAH-fuht)
an organization usually dedicated to addressing social issues

oceanographer (oh-shuh-NOG-ruh-fer)
a scientist who studies the ocean and ocean life

philanthropist (phil-AN-thro-pist)
a person who gives time or money to help others

pollution (puh-LOO-shuhn)
harmful materials that damage the environment

prototype (PROH-toh-tipe)
the first version of a new invention from which other versions are developed

READ MORE

Beer, Julie. *Kids vs. Plastic: Ditch the Straw and Find the Pollution Solution to Bottles, Bags, and Other Single-Use Plastics*. Washington, D.C.: National Geographic Children's Books, 2020.

French, Jess. *What a Waste: Trash, Recycling, and Protecting our Planet*. New York: DK Children, 2019.

Hamby, Rachel. *Saving the Oceans from Plastic*. Lake Elmo, MN: Focus Readers, 2020.

INTERNET SITES

The Ocean Cleanup
theoceancleanup.com

Plastic Oceans International
plasticoceans.org

TED Talks
ted.com/talks

INDEX